Contentment

Joy That Lasts

Resources for Changing Lives

A Ministry of
THE CHRISTIAN COUNSELING AND
EDUCATIONAL FOUNDATION
Glenside, Pennsylvania

RCL Ministry Booklets

Contentment

Joy That Lasts

Robert D. Jones

P&R
P U B L I S H I N G
P.O. BOX 817 • PHILLIPSBURG • NEW JERSEY 08865-0817

Italics within Scripture quotations indicate emphasis added.

Printed in the United States of America

Library of Congress Cataloging-in-Publication Data

Names: Jones, Robert D., 1959- author.
Title: Contentment : joy that lasts / Robert D. Jones.
Description: Phillipsburg, NJ : P&R Publishing Company, [2019] | Includes bibliographical references.
Identifiers: LCCN 2019006152 | ISBN 9781629956640 (pbk.) | ISBN 9781629956657 (epub) | ISBN 9781629956664 (mobi)
Subjects: LCSH: Contentment--Religious aspects--Christianity. | Joy--Religious aspects--Christianity. | Happiness--Religious aspects--Christianity.
Classification: LCC BV4647.C7 J66 2019 | DDC 248.4--dc23
LC record available at https://lccn.loc.gov/2019006152

One of my midlife delights is my grandchildren. What a joy it was to hold my two-hour-old granddaughter for an hour or so in the birthing center while my wife and son attended to my daughter-in-law in her delivery room. I simply stared at her nonstop, whispering my love for her and thanking God for the precious gift that she was. The ensuing months brought similar happy times. To look at this little treasure as she smiled and cooed was to glimpse a splendid picture of contentment!

Or so I thought. She's content . . . until she gets hungry or needs a diaper change or doesn't get what she wants. Then her so-called contentment evaporates instantly.

Thankfully, the kind of contentment that God promises does not disappear when circumstances sour. His contentment lasts even through hardship. It's not "contentment until" things go wrong but "contentment despite" things that are wrong. A far more accurate picture of contentment than a baby is an old, weather-beaten, hungry apostle who is languishing in a Roman dungeon—and yet singing praise to Christ his Redeemer. Listen to the apostle Paul's powerful, real-life testimony in Philippians 4:11–13.

> I have learned to be content whatever the circumstances. I know what it is to be in need, and I know what it is to have plenty. I have learned the secret of being content in any and every situation, whether well fed or hungry, whether living in plenty or in want. I can do all this through him who gives me strength.

We discover from this passage three takeaway principles about contentment.

1. You can learn true contentment.
2. You can enjoy true contentment despite hard circumstances.
3. You can find true contentment in God and nowhere else.

In the pages that follow, we will take a closer look at each of these principles before laying out a plan of daily steps we can take on the road to contentment. As you begin, note that we must not take these steps alone or in isolation from other believers. God has designed his church to contain pastors, elders, and other mature brothers and sisters who can teach you, encourage you, model for you, pray for you, and challenge you to grow in this fruit of Christian contentment. Consider strategic ways to involve these other people on your journey so that they can help you.

Three Principles of True Contentment

What is true contentment? The contentment that God gives is inner satisfaction in God alone, whatever the circumstances. A contented person experiences God's peace even in difficult times and consciously enjoys the fact that God is good no matter what. Contentment is the opposite of grumbling, complaining, and ingratitude. And it's more than passive acceptance, stoic resignation, or an attempt to grin and bear it or white-knuckle it through adversity. In the words of Puritan minister Jeremiah Burroughs, contentment is "that sweet, inward, quiet, gracious frame of spirit, which freely submits to and delights in God's wise and fatherly disposal in every situation."[1]

To be content, you must positively pursue and actively experience the deeper, lasting joy that Jesus Christ brings. Let's begin with the first principle we found in Philippians 4.

Principle 1: You Can Learn True Contentment

Here is God's good news for you: amid all your problems and pressures, you can indeed learn to become content. God guarantees it.

How do we find contentment? Does it float down from heaven so that we wake up one morning with it? Does it come from a trip down a church aisle to some altar? Do we exorcise demons of discontent in order to get it? Must we "pray through" it properly, perform some one-time act of "fully yielding" to the Lord, or receive a mystical spiritual gift?

The answer is no. You don't receive or discover contentment; you *learn* it! Paul explains, "I have learned to be content. . . . I have learned the secret of being content" (Phil. 4:11–12). Contentment is not a mystery to uncover but a mindset to cultivate. It arises from a process of Christian growth.

In his description of this process, Paul uses two different Greek terms for "learn." The first term carries the sense of learning something experientially—grasping the truth personally and living it out practically. It's the same verb that Hebrews 5:8 uses to recall that Jesus "learned obedience from what he suffered." This doesn't mean that Jesus didn't know intellectually that he should obey his Father or that there existed in him some prior state of disobedience. It means that he needed to learn *experientially*—at each moment—to obey God in the crucible of suffering. Similarly, when Titus 3:14 calls God's people to "learn to devote themselves to doing what is good," we don't doubt that they intellectually knew that they should do good works. But they needed to put into practice the priorities and habits of doing good to others. In the same way, Paul had to learn experientially how to find contentment moment-by-moment in the Lord even when he faced a host of hardships.

The second term that Paul uses for "learn" is a rarer verb that was used in his surrounding culture to signal initiation into some secret society or mystery religion. In this context, Paul Christianizes the term in order to remind us that entrance into the sphere of Christian contentment requires intentional, dedicated commitment.

Horatio Spafford's famous hymn mightily underscores this.

> When peace, like a river, attendeth my
> way,
> When sorrows like sea billows roll;
> Whatever my lot, Thou hast taught me
> to say,
> It is well, it is well, with my soul.

Spafford wrote this hymn following the sudden, tragic death of his four daughters. As he saw in his own life, whether our lot brings flowing tranquility or billowing sorrows, God teaches us ("Thou hast *taught* me") contentment. The second stanza deepens the point.

Though Satan should buffet, though trials should come,
Let this blest assurance control,
That Christ has regarded my helpless estate,
And hath shed his own blood for my soul.[2]

We can withstand Satan and trials, but only if gospel truths—Christ's death for us while we were in the helpless condition of sin—*control* our minds. That's part of the progressive, inner-person transformation of Christian maturity.

Principle 2: You Can Enjoy True Contentment Despite Hard Circumstances

It's one thing for God to assure us that we can learn contentment. But is that possible when our hardships oppose our happiness?

God's good news continues with our second principle. Not only is contentment learnable and something you can experience, but it is something you can experience even when hardships hit. Your spiritual happiness does not depend on your life happenings. Notice the comprehensiveness of Paul's words: "I have learned to be content *whatever* the circumstances. I know what it is *to be in need*, and I know what it is *to have plenty*. I have learned the secret of being content *in any and every situation*, whether *well fed* or *hungry*, whether living *in plenty* or *in want*" (Phil. 4:11–12). No possible experience is excluded from this.

Such expansive and inclusive language might sound too good to be true—hyper-spiritualized God-talk. But Paul was no mere theorist or ivory-tower philosopher. He wrote these words from prison, amid severe adversity. This man lived out the lessons that he taught. Paul was a real person facing real problems, and he practiced what he preached. He learned contentment—that "sweet, inward, quiet, gracious frame of spirit" that Burroughs describes.

As we seek to grasp the breadth of the contentment that Paul had learned, "whatever the circumstances" and "in any and every situation," let's consider seven hardships that he faced and the similar trials we sometimes encounter.

Financial pressures. Perhaps you find it hard to make ends meet each month, leaving you with little hope of a positive cash flow or future savings. In Philippians 4:11–12, Paul recalls times of hunger and poverty that were far worse than what most of us have faced. In 2 Corinthians 6, he describes the paradox of being "known, yet regarded as unknown; dying, and yet we live on; beaten, and yet not killed; sorrowful, yet always rejoicing; poor, yet making many rich; having nothing, and yet possessing everything" (vv. 9–10; see also

2 Cor. 11:27). Paul owned nothing materially—but everything spiritually. It's no wonder that he encouraged Timothy by saying,

> But godliness with contentment is great gain. For we brought nothing into the world, and we can take nothing out of it. But if we have food and clothing, we will be content with that. (1 Tim. 6:6–8)

Donna and Jason were surprised by their pregnancy and rejoiced in the birth of their baby. Both were committed to Donna being a stay-at-home mom, while knowing that she could pick up some occasional part-time work. But they were not ready for the financial challenges that came with their decision. As they entered the world of young parenthood, they found themselves becoming jealous of those in their church who had more money. They also dealt with various forms of guilt—Jason felt guilty that he couldn't provide a better salary, and Donna felt guilty that she no longer contributed in substantial ways to the family income. They struggled with anger toward the Lord for the dilemma they faced and with an assortment of worries and fears. Thankfully, as believers, through the truths we will see below, they began to experience the kind of contentment that Paul expressed above.

I think of another Christian couple who struggled to make ends meet and yet often invited my wife and me over for a meal. "Nothing fancy," they would assure us. Then, with a smile, they would add, "We'll find some dry bread and soup to serve." We caught their allusion to Proverbs 17:1: "Better a dry crust with peace and quiet than a house full of feasting, with strife." Meals with them were certainly peaceful. They understood Philippians 4.

Physical illness and injury. Few hardships challenge our contentment more than physical suffering does. Maybe you've suffered an injury. Perhaps you face ongoing bodily problems that discourage you—especially if they are incurable and degenerative. The apostle Paul, himself, was hardly a picture of health. He suffered a severe illness (perhaps malaria), which sidelined him from his work and interrupted his ministry plans (see Gal. 4:13–14). He was beaten five times with whips and three times with rods, suffered three or four shipwrecks, and was stoned so severely by his enemies that people presumed he was dead (see Acts 14:19; 2 Cor. 11:23–29).

Paul was aware of the temptations that come with bodily problems—the same temptations that we face: to question, doubt, or pull away from God, to pull away from others, to demand that others serve us, to wallow in depression, and so on. Yet these and other bodily problems—even seemingly chronic ones—did not prevent Paul from experiencing contentment. In 2 Corinthians 4:7–18, he detailed how his outer man—his bodily jar of clay—was wasting away. Yet he didn't despair over his physical decay, because he knew that the Lord Jesus was manifesting his life through Paul. Paul knew that God would raise him from the dead. And he knew that God was using Paul's suffering to renew and strengthen his inner man.

Have you met people like that? One of the most meaningful duties I had as a full-time pastor was to minister to hospitalized church members. On many occasions I visited older, seasoned Christians with the purpose of encouraging them, only to find them encouraging and loving me. "Who just ministered to whom?" I would think to myself, wondering why they hadn't followed the script I had arrogantly assumed they should follow. These were men and women whose attitude of ministering to others emerged from a contentment that was far deeper than their illness. They also realized, as Paul taught a little earlier in Philippians, that "our citizenship is in heaven. And we eagerly await a Savior from there, the Lord Jesus Christ, who, by the power that enables him to bring everything under his control, will transform our lowly bodies so that they will be like his glorious body" (Phil. 3:20–21).

Undesired singleness. I hesitate to include singleness in our list, since Paul didn't view it as problematic. Nevertheless, singleness likely offered him occasions for discontent. He lacked the companionship, comfort, and consolation that a life partner brings. Moreover, since Paul likely had been married at one time (as a former exemplary Pharisee—see Phil. 3:5), he likely suffered the loss of his wife through death or divorce. Yet he learned contentment in every circumstance—including his single status. (In fact, he even found this state preferable—see 1 Cor. 7.)

Not everyone, however, handles singleness so well. Maybe you long to marry or remarry, but you find that window closing and the prospect of a lifetime of singleness becoming more probable. Many singles allow their status to paralyze them with loneliness, anger against God and others, self-centeredness, immorality, jealousy, and despair. Additional complications come when singleness results from a broken engagement or marriage. Yet the message of the gospel is clear: whatever the cause of your single status—whether you were never married, widowed, or divorced—if you believe in Christ, you are a son or daughter of God and an heir of his promises (see

Gal. 3:26–29). Even if your friends or church members don't fully know you or understand you, Jesus does. He can provide you with inner satisfaction.

Throughout our thirty-five years of pastoral and counseling ministry, my wife and I have known dozens of single men and women who have learned the contentment that Jesus brings—friends like Meredith, in her late thirties, whose intimate relationship with Christ, close companionship with her Christian brothers and sisters, and active ministry to others bring her more fulfillment than many married couples have whom we know.

Memories of a sinful past. Do you live with ongoing guilt over your past sins? Maybe your past failures haunt you. Something that you said or did—or failed to say or do—troubles you. Perhaps it was a single incident or perhaps a pattern of behavior. Maybe you found some initial forgiveness, but it hasn't stuck; maybe you never did.

In 1 Timothy 1:12–17, Paul recalled his unsavory past as a blasphemer, persecutor, and violent man. Yet these memories didn't prevent him from experiencing God-given contentment. Paul didn't seek to forget or erase his past. Instead, he reinterpreted the memories he had of that past.[3] He saw them as constant reminders of God's forgiving grace and mercy.

By God's grace, they became an occasion for Paul to praise God—to bear witness to God's immense patience with and mercy toward sinners—and this became part of Paul's message to others. His past memories became current opportunities for Paul to deal with his sinful past in God's way and to live out his new identity as a fully forgiven son of God.

Kenny, a fellow church member, shared with me his shameful past, which included several forms of sexual sin with several different partners. While we rejoiced in his recent conversion to Christ, this didn't automatically remove those memories. Despite his efforts to rid himself of those remembrances—which included several rounds of professional therapy—he couldn't shake them. It was only when he began to grasp and apply the gospel—God's forgiving and cleansing grace—to his past and his present that he was able to rest in the Lord and find true joy each day.

Job hardships. Maybe you feel burdened by an unbearable job. You wonder whether you're in the right career. Maybe you're unemployed or are merely surviving an unstable or dead-end job. Or perhaps you are facing retirement due to disability or aging.

Paul faced a range of vocational problems. He carried the heavy weight—"the daily pressure"—of pastoral concern for the health of many churches and many individuals (see 2 Cor. 11:28; see also 1 Thess. 3:5). This was doubly worse for churches whose members suffered conflict (see Rom. 14; Phil. 4:2–3), false teaching (see Col. 2), or doctrinal defection (see Gal. 1). His concern for others rested relentlessly on his shoulders. Even as he wrote his letter to the Philippians, his career was on hold—and ready to be halted forever—as he sat in prison, unjustly accused and awaiting execution. Talk about job uncertainty.

Several months ago, a hardworking friend lost his position due to a sudden act of company downsizing. When I asked him about it, he spoke graciously about the company and expressed no words of resentment. He was grateful for the time he had been able to work there and for the experience and paychecks he had gained. And he saw this development as a fresh opportunity to draw near to the Lord and trust him for the next steps. He knew that inner satisfaction came not from his job but from his God.

Opposition and persecution from unbelievers. Do non-Christians oppose you because of your faith? Paul faced opposition—sometimes violent opposition—wherever he went. He learned contentment despite persecution, imprisonment, and death threats from unbelievers. Comparing himself to the false teachers who were corrupting the Corinthian church, Paul wrote,

> I have worked much harder, been in prison more frequently, been flogged more severely, and been exposed to death again and again. Five times I received from the Jews the forty lashes minus one. Three times I was beaten with rods, once I was pelted with stones, three times I was shipwrecked, I spent a night and a day in the open sea, I have been constantly on the move. I have been in danger from rivers, in danger from bandits, in danger from my fellow Jews, in danger from Gentiles; in danger in the city, in danger in the country, in danger at sea; and in danger from false believers. (2 Cor. 11:23–26)

Yet none of these many hardships stripped Paul of his joy. Amid hostility, he rested in God as his refuge, protector, and provider. How else can we explain his prison experience in Philippi, when, having been severely flogged, he was still "praying and singing hymns to God" (Acts 16:25)?

While Christians in the West rarely suffer physical persecution for their faith, our brothers and sisters in other places do. And believers in the United States do face other forms of opposition. Ask the student who carries his Bible to school or offers a Christian perspective in a classroom discussion. Ask the Christian wife who refuses to participate in her husband's illegal activity. Ask the office worker who expresses discomfort with crude humor or conversations that belittle others.

Or ask the Christian university professor who is bypassed for a department chair post because he is not sufficiently tolerant of diverse views. J. I. Packer describes such a person: "I walked in the sunshine with a scholar who had effectively forfeited his prospects of academic advancement by clashing with church dignitaries over the gospel of grace. 'But it doesn't matter,' he said at length, 'for I've known God and they haven't.' The remark was a mere parenthesis, a passing comment on something I said, but it has stuck with me and set me thinking."[4] Knowing God brings us contentment in all sorts of scenarios.

Rejection from believers. Let's consider one more form of suffering, which is perhaps the most painful: being misunderstood or abandoned by your friends. Later in Philippians 4, Paul recalled how every church but one had forgotten him (see v. 15). His coworker John Mark had deserted him (see Acts 15:38). Near the end of his life, Paul lamented that "everyone in the province of Asia has deserted me.

. . . Demas . . . has deserted me. . . . At my first defense, no one came to my support, but everyone deserted me" (2 Tim. 1:15; 4:10, 16). Nevertheless, he found contentment. How so? He knew he was not alone: "The Lord stood at my side and gave me strength" (2 Tim. 4:17).

In 2 Corinthians 6:11–13, Paul expresses what might be his most passionate emotional appeal. You can see his tears and feel his pain as you read his words:

> We have spoken freely to you, Corinthians, and opened wide our hearts to you. We are not withholding our affection from you, but you are withholding yours from us. As a fair exchange—I speak as to my children—open wide your hearts also.

As sad as its might be, we should not be shocked if a fellow Christian deserts us. Paul, and every Christian who has faced rejection for his or her faith, is simply experiencing the same suffering that Jesus faced. To his disciples, on the very eve of his crucifixion, Jesus soberly predicted that "a time is coming and in fact has come when you will be scattered, each to your own home. You will leave me all alone" (John 16:32).

How crushing this must be! To know that in your impending hour of greatest need your closest friends will desert you—will leave you hanging, literally. Our Lord stuns us with what he says in the remainder of that verse: "Yet I am not alone"—how can a person who is about to be abandoned by every earthly friend say that he's not alone?—"for my Father is with me." There was an invisible presence that outweighed his friends' abandonment. Jesus knew the *reality* of being rejected by people—there is no denial or pretending in what he said—but he also knew the *greater reality* of being accepted by God. His Father's presence trumped everyone else's absence. He found lasting joy in this.

Learning contentment in cases like this requires you to contrast the reality of others' rejection of you with the reality of God's presence, acceptance, and comfort. Where will you place your weight? Whose acceptance do you most cherish? Whose rejection do you most fear? Which reality will control you?

Jillian had suffered so many episodes of rejection, from childhood through adulthood, that she could not even say the full word—she called it the "R word." She lamented how every member of her family, and every friend she had known, had abandoned her—even her Christian sisters and brothers. It was only through a renewed communion with the Lord and a deliberate (albeit difficult) effort to engage in healthy Christian community that she was able to slowly enjoy Philippians 4 contentment.

In our survey of these seven kinds of suffering that Paul faced and that you and I might face, one constant emerges. Whatever your circumstances—whether you struggle financially, suffer a bodily trial, are dissatisfied with your singleness (or your marriage), are unemployed, underemployed, or unhappily employed, are looked down on or opposed because of your faith, or feel slighted, bypassed, or abandoned by fellow believers—Jesus Christ can bring you contentment. In any and every situation, Jesus Christ provides contentment to those who trust and follow him.

Principle 3: You Can Find True Contentment in God and Nowhere Else

Realizing that a Christian can indeed learn contentment and can do so even when facing a broad range of suffering leads to the next question: How? How did Paul gain contentment? From what or whom did it come? The answer is simple but deep—clear yet profound. Paul found contentment in his God. Contentment comes not from your circumstances but from your Savior. It flows from your heavenly Father.

Listen to the apostle's explicitly godward testimony in Philippians 4. He begins with a

"Therefore" in verse 1 that reminds us of our heavenly citizenship and of the Lord's promise to return and complete the salvation that he began, which were discussed in the final verses of the previous chapter. He states that he found joy "in the Lord" (v. 4) and in knowing that "the Lord is near" (v. 5). He found hope in "the peace of God" (v. 7) and "the God of peace" (v. 9). He found the power to live, above his bad circumstances, "through him who gives me strength" (v. 13). God promises us true contentment, and Paul himself was a walking example of this.

Above all, consider Jesus himself. No one before or since has suffered the intense abuse that he suffered: ridicule, rejection, physical torture, abandonment, unjust beatings, and more—all of which he suffered as an entirely innocent man who sought only and always to love his oppressors. Yet, in the midst of it all, he entrusted himself to God the Father and found inward peace and joy.

In both of these cases, Paul's and Jesus's contentment came from God. This contentment flowed, as Philippians 4 shows us, from God's joy, nearness, peace, and provisions.

Yet we notice in Philippians 4:13 how Paul highlights one specific attribute of God: his power. The apostle connects contentment specifically to God's strength: "I can do all this [i.e., live contentedly] through him who gives me strength." Paul echoes this in 1 Timothy 1:12: "I thank Christ Jesus our Lord, who has given me strength." And in 2 Timothy 4:17, he recalls a time of trial when "the Lord stood at my side and gave me strength." When faced with severe circumstances, you must be convinced that the Lord himself is standing at your side to impart supernatural strength.

Paul learned contentment as he learned to rely on God's mighty presence, even in the midst of difficult circumstances. While we don't know whether Paul's "thorn in the flesh" (see 2 Cor. 12:7–10) was a painful medical condition or a metaphor for enemy persecution, Paul pleaded with the Lord to remove it. While he didn't grant Paul's request, the Lord guaranteed something greater: his all-sufficient, enabling grace—his sustaining power. "My grace is sufficient for you, for my power is made perfect in weakness" (2 Cor. 12:9).

How did Paul respond? He found comfort and even delight in the Lord. He felt God's power come upon him—"that Christ's power may rest on me." As he humbled himself before the Lord, he discovered God's enabling grace: "For when I am weak, then I am strong" (vv. 9–10). Paul's strength came from the Lord—through his faith in God's ability to help him, despite difficulty. The result was confidence ("I will boast"—v. 9) and joy ("I delight"—v. 10; "gladly"—v. 9)—dual marks of contentment.

You discover God's power when you are conscious of your powerlessness. As one cancer-suffering friend put it, "The sense of weakness and need is a gift from God. It makes us realize that we need him, that we need all of his mercy to us, and that we need people who love us." Your weakness is the doorway into God's presence.

This truth about contentment amid weakness pops up all over the Bible. Joseph, in Genesis 37, 39–50, learned contentment despite a history of mistreatment from his teen years into his adulthood. When we trace his story we find God's presence, power, and sovereignty upholding him. In Psalm 46, the psalmist experienced peace and joy amid earthquake-like stressors, precisely because of God's ever-present, strong help. Habakkuk 3 provides an amazing example of contentment. The prophet envisioned horrific famine: "the fig tree does not bud and there are no grapes on the vines . . . the olive crop fails and the fields produce no food . . . there are no sheep in the pen and no cattle in the stalls" (v. 17). His response to this? "Yet I will rejoice in the Lord, I will be joyful in God my Savior" (v. 18). What produced this unexpected response? "The Sovereign Lord is my strength; he makes my feet like the feet of a deer, he enables me to tread on the heights" (v. 19).

The pattern here replicates Philippians 4—

(1) amid hard circumstances, (2) we can find contentment, peace, and joy (3) as we depend on the Lord who gives us strength. We will find Christian contentment in our trials only when we look to almighty God to give us the strength to believe his promises, to rest in his provisions, to recall our heavenly citizenship, and to follow his commands. Contentment comes when those who belong to Jesus rely on God's powerful presence in the face of life's trials.

I love the story of the dad who asked his young son to lift a very heavy object—a task that was far beyond the little boy's ability. The object would not budge. "Try again, son." The boy tried again with no success. "Son, you're not using all your strength." The boy tried again, but still it would not move. "Son, you're still not using all your strength." "Oh, daddy, daddy; I'm trying, I'm trying," grunted the boy as he strained at the immovable object. "I'm using all my strength." "No you're not, son," replied the father. "You haven't asked *me* to help!"

Returning to Philippians 4, we find that the key to contentment lies with God. Stoic philosophers in Paul's day used the same Greek term that is translated "content" in Philippians 4:11–12 to indicate self-sufficiency. They taught that people have innate strength to endure trials—the same philosophy that we daily hear in our own world: "You are the master of your fate—the captain of your soul. Be tough. Be a rock. Be your own dog!" The apostle, however, takes the same Stoic term and reframes it for the Christian. He fills it with Christ. Contentment is based not on self-sufficiency but on God-sufficiency. Paul's life was dependent on Jesus, not on his own abilities or character (see Phil. 1:21; 3:10).

Why is this distinction so important? Because our culture calls people to be self-sufficient, not God-sufficient. The media, educators, and government leaders, along with athletes, artists, and actors, all unite to feed us lies. They tell our children, "Success lies in your hands. Reach for the sky. Be all you can be. Your potential knows no limits. It's yours for the taking." Television cameras highlight celebrities who visit inner-city schools in order to tell kids that if they stay in school and say no to drugs, "You can be whatever you want to be." As Christians, we certainly encourage children to live drug-free and to aspire to achieve productive lives. Yet we recoil at the self-sufficiency that this message engenders. The Bible rejects all arrogance and any presumption that excludes God, ignores him or, at best, merely politely acknowledges him.

Dear friend, the apostle, like you, endured his share of suffering. Yet he found contentment. But he didn't find it in his circumstances; he found it in his God. Period.

Three Daily Steps to Learn True Contentment

What specific steps can we take to learn contentment?

1. Know and Embrace the Bible's Truths about God

In order to learn contentment, you must first know and embrace the Bible's truths about God's character, presence, and promises. You must know who God is and what he is like. This includes knowing that he is good, despite the bad circumstances that you face. You must start with sound doctrine—not your experience or the opinions of others. Renew your mind with Scripture. Start with Romans 8:28–39 and realize that its promises are given to believers like you, who suffer and groan in this fallen world. Meditate on chapters 1 and 2 of Ephesians—a letter that was written to former pagans who had their share of past and present sin and misery. Understand, from 1 Peter 1, that Christ redeemed you "from the empty way of life handed down to you from your ancestors" (v. 18).

Consider the teenager whose dad divorces his mother and, in doing so, essentially divorces his son. How can that Christian young man find contentment? He must know that God is with him, that God loves him, that God will help him to handle this trial, and that God will use it to make him more like Jesus—the ultimate good that Romans 8:28–29 teaches.

The key to learning contentment in God is to focus not on your learning activity but on God himself, as he has revealed himself in Christ as our Redeemer.

Do you recall that old adage "To know me is to love me"? We use it to encourage others to trust us or be patient with us. How many times have you thought to yourself, "If So-and-so really knew me, they'd like me and believe me" and so on? In a very real sense, learning contentment begins with hearing God say, "To know me is to love me. If you can see me as I am, if you can grasp my grace and believe my promises, you will find your contentment in me."

2. Identify and Repent of Lies You Have Believed

In order to learn contentment, you must next identify and repent of the lies you have unknowingly imbibed and the false foundations on which you have vainly sought contentment. Identify the various ways—both obvious and subtle—in which you have pursued contentment in things, people, and experiences. How have you trusted in yourself and in your own strength, wisdom, and endurance? Label these things for what they are—lies and idols. Then determine, with God's help, to cease pursuing these false objects of trust and to turn instead to God and his truth.

One practical way to identify these false foundations is to honestly answer these diagnostic questions: "What do I believe would make me content? What would need to happen?" If your answer involves some change of circumstance or some improved relationship, then that thing is now functioning as your source of contentment—if you have it, you will be happy; if you lack it, you will be crushed with despair. You are a yo-yo on a string—this thing has you in its grasp and can raise you up and down at its will. It is an idol functioning as your god.

For example, if your contentment hinges on finding a spouse or on getting married, then it's not based on Christ. If your contentment will come only if your spouse or friend treats you better or if you receive some financial blessing, physical healing, or human applause, then it is not Christ-based contentment. You are building your life on shifting sand. God never meant for you to find lasting joy in anything other than Christ himself. I pray that you won't.

Conversely, if contentment is indeed independent of your circumstances, then you must not look to improved circumstances to bring you comfort. Good things do not guarantee true happiness. Identify and reject these competing gods—the Lord God requires exclusive allegiance. Then bow to him who sent Jesus to save sinners like you and me. Ask him to teach you what it means to rejoice in him and to learn his contentment amid your hardships. Christian contentment will elude you until you renounce its counterfeits.

3. Apply God's Word to Your Situation

Finally, in order to learn contentment you must practically, actively, and progressively apply God's Word to your current situation—and especially to your hardships. "Great peace" says the psalmist, "have those who love your law, and nothing can make them stumble" (Ps. 119:165). "Blessed is the one . . . whose delight is in the law of the LORD, and who meditates on his law day and night" (Ps. 1:1–2). The book of Philippians, which is packed with present and future promises, would be a good place to start.

One helpful memory aid to consider is the PTO acrostic (Pray, Think, Obey) that is drawn from Philippians 4:6–9—pray in various ways (see vv. 6–7); think about godly, virtuous things (which, in this situation, might mean focusing on various biblical truths—see v. 8), and obey God's truth (see v. 9). Seeking God's face, renewing your mind with his truth, and walking in his ways will produce inner peace (see vv. 6, 9) despite your circumstantial problems. Ask God to help you to cling to his grace and rest on his promises.

Along with reading and reflecting on Scripture, many people whom my wife and I have counseled have found Christ-centered music to be an aid in their fight for joy. One woman summarized it well: "Songs minister to me greatly. I think that I'm drawn to those that talk about who God is and his promises, as well as pointing my heart toward worship and getting my eyes toward Jesus and off me." She proceeded to list several hymns that burst with God's attributes and assurances. Perhaps none speak of contentment more powerfully than "Be Thou My Vision"—especially in its third stanza:

> Riches I heed not, nor man's empty praise
> Thou mine inheritance, now and always
> Thou and Thou only first in my heart
> High King of heaven, my Treasure Thou Art.[5]

In a discussion of contentment, Jerry Bridges offers a grace-centered perspective that can help us to renew our minds: "First, we must learn to live by the realization that whatever our situation might be, it is far better than we deserve. Actually, we deserve God's eternal judgment. It's been said, 'Anything this side of hell is pure grace.' This statement is true, and we must accept it and adjust our attitude accordingly."[6] In other words, however bad your circumstances are, they are better than what you deserve!

I vividly recall the first time this truth smacked me in the face, when I was a young pastor, and forced me to "adjust my attitude accordingly." It was a hot July day. I was carrying two armloads of Philippians commentaries and other reference books from my home office to my church office across the street. As I reached the door, my arms ready to break, I expected to find it opened, as it often is during the day. Alas—it was locked! That meant that I had to set the books down at the door and go home to get my keys. In the midst of my frustration, about to yell, I remembered this truth: "However bad your circumstances are, they are better than what you deserve. Bob, you deserve hell—not a life of ease and open doors. You deserve something worse than this July heat, and yet God in Christ has mercifully spared you from his wrath and made you his son." The incident was minor—an inconvenience not worthy to be called suffering. Yet God drove this principle home through that small situation, and he has reminded me of it in more serious trials ever since.

These, then, are the three steps toward learning contentment: (1) growing in your knowledge of God and his promises, (2) identifying and repenting of the false foundations on which you have built your happiness, and (3) progressively applying God's truth as you pray, think biblically, and obey God's Word.

Holly, a thirty-six-year-old Christian homemaker, had to learn this pathway of faith and repentance. Marriage frustrations brought her to counseling. Her communication with her husband ranged from nonexistent to volatile. Motherhood had failed to fulfill her dreams, and she daily lived with the lingering sense that "there must be more out there for me." Thankfully, by God's grace, she came to see that the problem lay not with her husband or with her status as a homemaker. By reflecting on Philippians 4, she began to see how she had sought contentment not in Christ and his present and future promises but in her marital and motherly ideals. She had believed the Evil One's lies that happiness consisted in a changed husband and had allowed that legitimate desire to become a ruling reality—the functional god that controlled her and that she thought would fulfill her. As she identified and confessed these ruling demands and wrong expectations, God began to liberate her. The Lord re-set her identity as his daughter, and he forgave and empowered her to live a new life of true contentment.

Two Contrasting Pictures

I began this booklet with a common way in which many people picture contentment: the smiling, cooing baby. But we saw how temporal, circumstantial, and fickle this type of contentment is. Take away the baby's bottle while she's drinking, or her favorite toy that she's holding, and what happens? All her contentment vanishes. Pick her up or set her down when she doesn't want to be picked up or set down, and your content "coo-er" quickly becomes an inconsolable "waa-er." A baby's so-called contentment depends on her having favorable circumstances. Infant contentment is untested; when tried by hardship or disappointment, it disappears.

As we have seen, the apostle Paul—imprisoned, hungry, and weather-beaten—gives us a much more accurate picture of contentment. Take away Paul's bottle or his favorite toy, and he still finds joy in Jesus! Pick him up or set him down when he doesn't want you to, and instead of a temper tantrum, he prays for you and blesses you. The apostle has learned contentment despite severe hardships. Contentment does not depend on circumstances.

Reader, contentment is that condition of consciously enjoying God's goodness, whatever your circumstances. It is the ability to live a satisfied, God-pleasing life in any and every situation. The apostle Paul learned how to do this, despite an array of afflictions—financial problems; bodily illnesses, accidents, and injuries; singleness and family problems; memories of past sin; job problems; persecution, imprisonment, and death threats from unbelievers; and misunderstanding, rejection, and abandonment by his own friends.

Paul learned contentment, and so can you!

May God—the God who powerfully provides for and empowers all who trust in Christ—help you to learn the lessons that his suffering apostle learned, no matter how hard your circumstances may be. Let's find lasting contentment in him who loved us and gave himself up for us on the cross.

Robert D. Jones *(MDiv; DMin; DTheol) is a biblical counseling professor at The Southern Baptist Theological Seminary in Louisville, Kentucky, and has served in pastoral ministry for over thirty years.*

Notes

1 Jeremiah Burroughs, *The Rare Jewel of Christian Contentment* (repr., Carlisle, PA: Banner of Truth, 1992), 19. For an abridged version that is easier to read, see Jeremiah Burroughs, *Learning to Be Happy* (repr., London: Grace Publications, 2011).

2 Horatio G. Spafford, "It Is Well with My Soul," 1876.

3 For a fuller unpacking of this passage and application of it to this problem, see Robert D. Jones, *Bad Memories: Getting Past Your Past* (Phillipsburg, NJ: P&R, 2004).

4 J. I. Packer, *Knowing God* (Downers Grove, IL: InterVarsity Press, 1973), 20.

5 "Be Thou My Vision," trans. Mary E. Byrne, 1905, versed Eleanor H. Hull, 1912.

6 Jerry Bridges, *The Practice of Godliness* (Colorado Springs: NavPress, 1983), 121.

RCL Ministry Booklets

Booklets by Jeffrey S. Black, Michael R. Emlet, Walter Henegar, Robert D. Jones, Susan Lutz, James C. Petty, David Powlison, Darby Strickland, Paul David Tripp, Edward T. Welch, and John Yenchko.

ADD
Anger
Angry at God?
Bad Memories
Contentment
Depression
Domestic Abuse
Forgiveness
God's Love
Guidance
Homosexuality
"Just One More"
Marriage
Motives
OCD
Pornography
Pre-Engagement
Priorities
Procrastination
Prodigal Children
Self-Injury
Sexual Sin
Stress
Suffering
Suicide
Teens and Sex
Thankfulness
Why Me?
Why Worry?
Worry

See all the books and booklets in the Resources for Changing Lives series at www.prpbooks.com

More on Contentment

The world pressures us to fulfill our desires—but God tells us to master them through contentment. This practical daily devotional helps us cultivate thankfulness in situations that fuel discontent.

"A practical daily devotional full of how-to's and why-to's [and], more importantly . . . the 'who' of a daily relationship with Jesus Christ."
—David Murray, Puritan Reformed Theological Seminary

"With clear, practical, biblical reflection, Hill leads us to the greener pastures of Christian contentment."
—Jen Pollock Michel, *Teach Us to Want* and *Keeping Place*